Rhyming Fun with Billy and Trish

Poetry and Illustrations by

Ben Nuttall-Smith

Rhyming Fun With Billy and Trish

Index

2	BILLY'S BICYCLE	19	DADDY AND ME
3	SHOPPING	20	BIG GAME HUNTING
4	TANTRUM TYCOON	21	FAIRY CIRCLE
5	MISCHIEVOUS TEDDY	21	NURSE TRISH
6	BILLY'S BULLFROG	22	THE BIRTHDAY DRESS
7	THE WIGGLY FINGERS	23	POOR TRISH
8	A DAY AT THE ZOO	24	TRISH'S OWIE
9	TO GRANDPA'S HOUSE	25	CRAYONS
10	WHEN I GOT BORN	26	BLUE JEANS
11	TIGER	27	BILLY'S CAMERA
12	IN MY HIGH CHAIR	28	READING
13	GINGER THE CAT	29	MY TEACHER
14	INVITATION	30	CLOUDS
15	LITTLE TYRANT	31	THE LADDER
16	RED BOOTS	32	SEA SIDE
17	IN MY BATHTUB	33	CATHEDRAL CAT
18	RUNNING AWAY	34	ME AND MY CAT
19	WHEN I GO TO SCHOOL		

Billy and Trish

Copyright © Ben Nuttall-Smith 2021

Author/Illustrator: Ben Nuttall-Smith

Publisher: Rutherford Press

Author website: https://bennuttall-smith.ca

For information, contact:

    Rutherford Press,
    PO Box 648
    Qualicum Beach, BC, Canada V9K 1A0
    info@rutherfordpress.ca

    https://rutherfordpress.ca

Printed in the United States of America and Canada.
All rights reserved. No part of this book may be reproduced in whole or in part, materially or digitally, including photocopying, without the express written permission of the author or publisher.

    ISBN   # 978-1-988739-51-9

Billy's Bicycle

watch out! watch out! everybody stand aside!

'cause here comes Billy on a bicycle ride.

he's flying along just as fast as can be:

"hey! all you people, look at me."

straight down the sidewalk and into the park.

Mommy's in a dither. little dogs bark.

Daddy's running out of breath. as far as he can go!

"Keep pushing, Daddy. don't let go!"

SHOPPING

When we go shopping, my Mommy and me,

she buys all the groceries, like brown bread and tea

and liver and onions and, ooh! brockerly.

I buy what's important like ketchup and jam

and lic'rice and corn pops and apples and ham.

I buy cheezies and corn chips and red seedless grapes

and oodles of noodles and choc'lit and dates.

I buy sweet buns and ice cream and sweet apple jack.

Then, when we're finished, Mom puts mine all back.

TANTRUM TYCOON

two year old Trish has a terrible temper.
she's a tantrum tycoon when she's mad.

she can whip up a scream that's a green monster's dream.
and her face can turn blue - oh! she's sad!
just last week, little Trish lay awake from a dream,
and she started to yell and she started to scream.
Mr. Wilson came over and he told my dad
that to wake us all up was incredibly bad.
but her tears on the floor made a puddle so deep
that we all took her sailing and rocked her to sleep.

MISCHIEVOUS TEDDY

oh, how I wish Teddy would do as he's told;

he's awf'ly mischievous, I don't like to scold.

last night, he wrote crayon all over the wall,

Mommy was furious, blamed me for it all.

he tips over my milk and spills juice on the rug.

he even made Jennifer swallow a bug.

it just isn't fair that they blame it on me.

it's Teddy who's naughty. I wish they could see.

I'll have to make Teddy stand facing the wall,

and I won't let him leave 'til he owns up to all.

oh, how I wish Teddy would learn to be good,

and not do what he shouldn't, and do what he should.

Billy's Bullfrog

Billy caught a bullfrog. he kept it in a jar,

and fed it flies and spiders and would pet it by the hour.

Billy caught a garter snake down by the garden pool

and, though his dad forbade it, took both to Sunday school.

now, frogs and snakes are harmless; i'm sure you'll all agree.

so Billy took them from the jar for everyone to see.

he showed the snake to Betty Jane and she let out a scream.

next thing, two of the other girls began to make a scene.

the congregation sang a hymn of creatures great and small

and listened to a sermon about peace on earth for all.

the pastor spoke of children, of blessings, and of joys

and the happiness of parents and ... heavens! what's that noise?

Billy had a bullfrog and a baby garter snake.

but taking them to Sunday school was a very sad mistake.

THE WIGGLY FINGERS

when Billy's in bed and he can't get to sleep,

there are wiggly fingers that tickle his feet.

it's a wiggly monster all purple and red,

and he lives in a corner right under his bed.

Billy curls up real small and he shuts his eyes tight,

and then he is safe for the rest of the night.

he lies quite still and he won't make a peep,

his head under the covers until he's asleep.

page 7

A Day At The Zoo

there's nothing more fun than a day at the zoo,

where there's lions and tigers and elephants too.

there are monkeys and penguins and long necked giraffes,

and llamas and camels and hyenas that laugh.

we ride on a small train past rivers and lakes,

full of green alligators and hippos and snakes.

we see zebras and leopards and birds of all kinds,

and sad looking rhinos with dusty behinds.

we have hot dogs and ice cream, cotton candy and pop.

poor Daddy's run ragged; he's ready to drop.

and dear baby brother is making a fuss.

it's time to go home. better get on the bus.

oh Daddy! dear Daddy! can we please come again?

of course. but now hurry, it's starting to rain.

TO GRANDPA'S HOUSE

we're going on a ferry ride, as far, as far can be,

way up the coast to Grandpa's house at Sechelt-by-the-Sea.

we've packed the car with swimming suits and sandwiches and pop

but we won't be at Grandpa's house 'til after ten o'clock.

I hope he takes us hiking along the rocky shore.

we'll even swim and dig for clams and buy ice cream and more.

and then we'll have a campfire and he'll sing silly rhymes

and tell us funny stories of kids in olden times.

we're going on a ferry ride, as far, as far can be,

way up the coast to Grandpa's house at Sechelt-by-the-Sea.

we've packed the car with swimming suits and sandwiches and pop

but we won't be at Grandpa's house 'til after ten o'clock.

When I Got Born

when I got born on a long spring night
and the sun shone bright in the rain,
I didn't have a shirt and I had no teeth
and I didn't have a penny to my name.
I was very, very young. I didn't say a word,
though I could have had a lot to say.
I thought it would be better as my Mommy was close by,
and I didn't want to frighten her away.
I had no hair and I was very, very small
and my skin was all wrinkled and red.
I lay there very quiet and I gurgled at the lights
and I cooed, then I widdled in my bed.
then a nurse came along and she took me to a table.
she bathed me and she wrapped me up in blue.
then she held me by a window where some funny people waved.
so I burped and I bellowed loud and long.
next, they took me to my Mommy and she held me in her arms.
then she gave me what I wanted all along:
to be fed and to be held, to be loved and to be wanted.
and i'm growing, and I'm growing big and strong.

TIGER

    tiger, lurking in his crib,
   growling through the wooden bars,
  mewling for a cookie and a drink.
threw out all his baby toys,
his blanket, and his blocks,
even tossed poor Teddy bear away.
monkey standing at the railing,
banging, clapping with his bottle,
calling out for anyone to hear.
"someone, someone come and change me,
hold me for a while.
 babble silly nothings in my ear."
    pussy cat's asleep now,
    purring on his thumb.
        dreaming 'bout his animals at bay.
        tomorrow, fuzzy puppy dog,
        a wee lamb, or a fish.
                new adventures wake to meet the day.

IN MY HIGH CHAIR

I sit in my high chair
and splash in my food
and I throw it all over the floor.
then when it's all gone
I'll scream and I'll shout
and Nanny will bring me some more.
it's such fun to blow peas
from my mouth to the mat.
and if he comes close,
I'll dump milk on the cat.
he'll run from the kitchen,
'cause he doesn't like that.
oh, eating's such fun when you're me!

Ginger the Cat

Ginger is my pussy cat. he's very, very bright.

he can play on the piano and he goes to work each night.

Ginger often catches mice, when we are all asleep.

my Daddy says that's his job, it's how he earns his keep.

I love to carry Ginger. I love to stroke his fur.

and when I scratch behind his ears his motor starts to purr.

INVITATION

you're invited to my party!
we'll have games and pop and cake,
and we're going to have a movie
and a piñata to break.

there'll be sandwiches and ice cream
and a Punch and Judy show.
I'll open all my presents
just before it's time to go.

LITTLE TYRANT

oh, boy! can I scream!   oh, boy! can I yell!
I've the lungs of a tyrant, just as loud as a bell.
if you tell me I can't, I will show you I can.
and I'll blast out the eardrums of any old man,
or mother, or father, or brother, or aunt.
so you'd better think twice 'fore you tell me I can't.
if I don't get my way, or you smack my behind,
I'll set up such a ruckus, you'll go out of your mind.
but cuddle me gently and croon me a song.
I'll be happy and pleasant the whole evening long.

RED BOOTS

I jump around in puddles in my bright red boots.

and I'll splash anybody who comes by.

and if silly Betty-Jane comes to bother me again,

I won't care if I even make her cry.

'cause when she screams and yells,

she runs right home and tells.

then my Mommy comes and sends me to my bed.

but I won't say i'm sorry; I'll just wrinkle up my eyes.

'cause I like to have fun in my boots all shiny red.

In My Bathtub

when I swim in my bathtub with
Dudley and Jack
and the bubbles come up to my nose,
i'm ever so good as I float on my back
and the waterfall lands on my toes.
I've a tug in the harbour and ships standing by
with a shark set to gobble the crew.
I can squirt with my guns, or destroy with one cry,
and a plane can dive out of the blue.
then my bold, gallant duck, Captain Dudley by name,
will come to the rescue at sea.
and Jack, who's a diver, will guide the ships home
while i'm pulled from the tub to get dry.

Running Away

i'm running away just as fast as I can.

I've packed my own suitcase with cookies and jam.

there's some honey for Teddy and toffee for me.

and I won't come home 'til it's late as can be.

I just won't take a nap when it's middle of day.

why should I lie down when it's more fun to play?

I don't want a bath. and I won't wash my hair.

they can cry if they like when they see i'm not there.

they can call a policeman; just see if I care.

I've gone 'round the block now; my legs are quite sore.

so I'd better go home – it's a quarter past four.

WHEN I GO TO SCHOOL

when I go to school I'll be ever so smart.
I will do all my sums and I'll know them by heart.
I'll have read all my books by a quarter to three
and I'll sit up real straight just as good as can be.
ooh! I hardly can wait 'til i'm five and a half
and go on the school bus with Bob.

DADDY AND ME

my Daddy's sooo strong! he's as strong as can be.
he can lift up a board that's as big as a tree.
he hammers in nails and he hits them all straight.
we are building a fence with a big garden gate,
and a see-saw and a swing for my brother and me.
my Daddy's sooo strong! he's as strong as can be.

BIG GAME HUNTING

I creep through the jungle with my trusty spear,
listening for hungry lions and tigers prowling near.
in a slow moving river, huge alligators swim.
so I jump to the other side while never falling in.
there are monkeys in the trees and long green snakes.
great hunters are courageous; we have what it takes.
when we find ourselves in danger, we're always brave and strong.
that's why I brought my compass and a pocket knife along.
I've journeyed on for many months. I've trudged the trails alone.
"Billy! time for supper" ... i'm a thousand miles from home.

"coming!"

FAIRY CIRCLE

there's a circle in my garden
where the fairies dance around
if you listen very softly
you might hear the tinkling sound
of their laughter.

come and find them in the evening
as the dew falls to the ground.

NURSE TRISH

Trish is going to be a nurse. she has a cape and cap.

she put a sling on Billy's arm and bandaged up the cat.

the nurse is in, she'll see you now. but first, she'll take your pulse.

and here's a needle for your arm; you mustn't make a fuss.

the nurse will fix your aching head she'll also cure your ills.

but it's no fun with Billy 'cause he eats all the pills.

The Birthday Dress

Mommy and me are writing a letter
to thank Auntie Jean for the dress.
but how would she know that little girls grow
and i'm four and a half - more or less.
still, the dress is so pretty, I wish it would fit.
it was made for a girl half my size.
when I opened the box and saw the red ribbons,
it was really a lovely surprise.
so, we won't tell my auntie the dress is too small;
she would be so upset if she knew.
and we're making believe that it fits me just right.
Mommy says that's the right thing to do.
then, maybe one day, when my aunt comes to visit,
she'll see just how much I have grown.
and i'm saving that dress in a chest in my room
until I have a girl of my own.

POOR TRISH

poor Trish fell out of the apple tree,

banging her elbow and scraping her knee.

at first, she just sat to recover her breath.

and then, she discovered a rip in her dress.

Trish started to cry, "oh, what shall I do?"

"my mother will kill me. this dress is brand new."

just then, she noticed the blood on her arm,

so she let out a wail - a loud cry of alarm.

"oh, Mommy! oh, Mommy! I can't stand the pain."

"please make it all better. I won't climb again."

Mommy taped up her elbow, her knee, and her head.

then she kissed her all better and put her to bed.

poor Trish was quite sad 'cause she'd wanted to play,

but she'd been sent to bed for the rest of the day.

TRISH'S OWIE

ooh! ooh! I've got an owie! it's a big one on my knee.

I suppose you think it's funny, Billy! don't you laugh at me.

I wonder how you'd like it if I did the same to you.

I bet you'd run home crying. you know darn well that's true.

if you don't stop that grinning, I'll tell Mommy. wait and see.

and then she'll make you 'pologize because I hurt my knee.

CRAYONS

I've got some crayons - blue and red

and purple and yellow and green.

i'm going to make a picture -

the best you've ever seen.

I'll fill the page with pussy cats

and flowers and trees and sky.

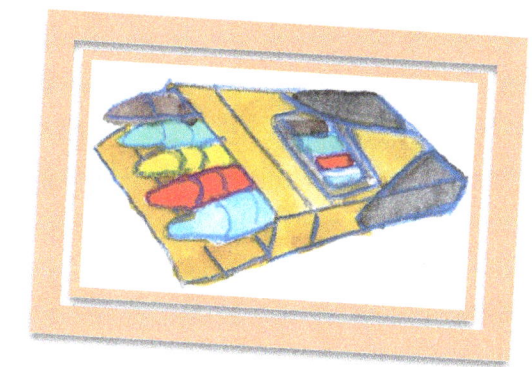

and Grandpa's house and his little red car

and white clouds floating by.

I'll draw you pretty ponies

and my Daddy strong and tall.

then, when my picture's finished,

you can put it on the wall.

BLUE JEANS

Trish has blue jeans and play shoes,

and she's learning the safe way to climb.

at last, Mommy knows

that you can't wear fine clothes

and still have an outdoors good time.

now, she swings on the rope swing with Billy,

and slides down the sand hill with Sue.

when a girl reaches four

she will tell you for sure

there's just nothing a person can't do.

Trish is saving her dresses for Sundays

and visits and parties and such.

she can run with the boys

making barrels of noise,

all the things she enjoys very much.

BILLY'S CAMERA

Billy's got a camera. everybody "cheeze!"

he lines his subjects up, just so, and gives a gentle squeeze.

he's photographed his Daddy and he photographed his Mom.

he commandeers us to the lawn and snaps us, one by one.

he has many shots of Teddy and of everyone he knows.

Billy always has his camera, no matter where he goes.

his photo skills are really good. one day he'll be a pro.

and, when he ever has some film, he'll have a lot to show.

READING

I can read real books.

listen everyone. "good dog Spot,

run Spot, run."

    I can read picture books

    "once upon a time...

don't interrupt me, Billy.

"run Spot, run."

    "in a land far away...

"see Spot jump.

    "there lived an old man...

Billy, go and play!

MY TEACHER

my teacher's Miss Temple and she's an old maid
and she lives with her cat, all alone.
oh, it would be so nice if she took our advice
and got married, had kids of her own.
she says there's no hurry. she's certain one day
her prince will arrive and he'll sweep her away
to a honeymoon island where sea urchins play.
but what will we do when she's gone?
Miss Temple is having a birthday
and my mother is baking a cake.
we're all making cards and bringing her flowers
because she will be twenty-eight.
and then, when school's over, she's leaving,
running off with a dentist from Rome.
but i'm glad I had her for my teacher
before she has kids of her own.

CLOUDS

there are angels in the blue sky.
do you see them, fluffy white?
I see a tiger.
there's a camel.
watch them charging!
what a sight!
there's an old man with a pink beard!
   I can see a pussy cat!
   baby angels fly so quickly
now he's picking up his hat.
   there are angels in the sunset.
   do you see them turning red?
watch the tiger eat the camel.

   come in children, time for bed.

THE LADDER

I can climb the ladder way up high.

see me reach out and touch the sky.

i'm up with the birds and the bumblebees.

Daddy, get the camera

and I'll smile "cheeze".

hey, everybody,

look at me.

i'm a giant,

big as can be.

time for cake and ice cream,

sandwiches and tea.

Mommy come.

help me down.

   one!

       two!

           three!

Sea Side

we're going to the sea side:
swimming suits, pails, spades,
picnic basket, blanket, folding chairs,
don't forget your sun hats and sun glasses.
everybody into the car!

v r o o o o m !

are we there yet? i'm thirsty. gotta' wee.
that was fun. too much sun.
did you see me swim, Daddy?
can we go again Daddy?
you've got a sun burn.
when'll we be home?
i'm thirsty.
gotta' wee.
are we home yet?

CATHEDRAL CAT

(cats occupy the upper levels of the Aya Sofya in Istanbul, Turkey)

my cat's gone away to sing in the choir
at a cathedral by the black sea.
I didn't know he was planning to go,
'til he made his announcement at tea.
he packed his pyjamas and toothbrush and comb,
and gave me a hug at the gate.
I whispered "goodbye", with a tear in my eye,
while he rushed off as though he were late.
I hope he enjoys the incredible noise,
though I've heard they put on quite a show.
still, it's terribly far to the "Aya-So-fya"
where the monks used to sing long ago.
they'll "meow" all night long, their sad pussycat song
then they'll feast on fresh catnip and mice.
while I'll miss the dear cat, I could not hold him back.
so a postcard will have to suffice.
my cat's gone to Turkey to sing in the choir,
and he won't be back home for a while.
but he sends me adventures and stories so fine,
and his anecdotes cause me to smile.

page 33

ME AND MY CAT

(all grow'd up)

we live on a hill in a big sunny house

and we stay in our house all alone.

just me and my cat

and we do as we like

and we like what we do

in our home.

we go to bed late

and we don't change our socks

and our clothes pile up on the floor.

he don't scream at me

and I don't yell at him

and he won't get upset if I snore.

if I can't eat my greens

and he won't drink his milk

we can still get dessert if we want.

'cause there's no one to say

that it's too late to play

so we can if we like

    but we won't.

THANK YOU SO MUCH FOR READING!

More books by Ben Nuttall-Smith are available at

Rutherford Press

https://rutherfordpress.ca

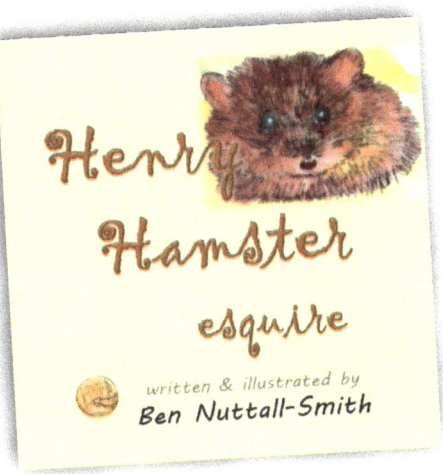

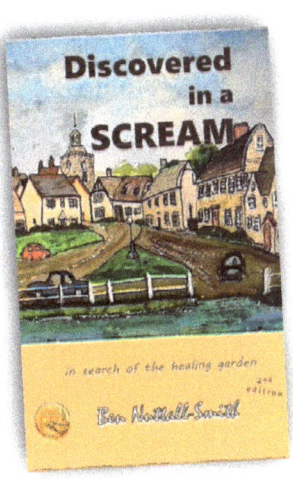